Philosophy for children

From child to children

Once upon a time!

The little boy's faith

From child to children

By: Bernardo Octaviano Pereira

This book belongs to:

____

I dedicate this work, firstly, to my parents who I love so much, to my teachers, to my dear aunts and to all my friends, may God bless you all infinitely!

Bernardo Octaviano Pereira

02/04/2024

Once upon a time, in a small country town, where the relentless sun punished the land that had been parched for a long time. An overwhelming drought was ravaging the region,

leaving behind withered crops, rivers that became beds of dust and animals suffering from lack of water.

The exhausted population seriously thought about abandoning the place they once called home.

That's when an important man had an idea. He had heard about a faith healer in the neighboring city, capable of performing true miracles, even making it rain.

They then decided to bring her to the city in the hope of reversing the situation.

The important man, armed with hope, gathered the people and announced the coming of the faith healer. Everyone contributed financially to bring what promised to return life to the land so thirsty.

The day came when the faith healer, with her mystical aura, presented herself in the center of the city, the healer with ceremonious gestures, uttered her prayers, crying out for divine mercy.

The news spread, and everyone was invited to gather in the central square to witness the faith healer in action. The women with their big hats and flowing dresses, the judge

imposing in his toga, the general with his shiny uniform and even the rich banker with his very expensive toothpick were present, everyone from the small town came to see the faith healer make it rain, expectations were high.

As she chanted her words, dark clouds began to form in the sky, and drops of rain, timid at first, began to fall, the rain that followed was not only a relief for the earth, but also a rebirth of hope for the whole city

However, among the crowd, only one little boy appeared carrying an umbrella. While everyone looked on skeptically, the little boy, with a gleam of faith in his eyes, believed that the blessing could bring the long-awaited rain.

Only this
little boy
had faith
that it
would rain.

The little boy with his umbrella open was smiling, because his faith had been rewarded. The city, now blessed by rain, saw a rebirth of hope and joy among residents.

The moral of the story is that, even in the most difficult situations, faith can be the flame that lights the path to a solution. Sometimes a child's belief is enough to make true miracles happen.

The end!